MW00814212

The Christmas Jokes for Kids Book

Over 250 Silly, Goofy, Knock Knock and Funny Holiday Jokes Perfect for Friends and Family at Any Christmas Party

DL Digital Entertainment

© COPYRIGHT 2019 - ALL RIGHTS RESERVED.

The content contained within this book may not be reproduced, duplicated or transmitted without direct written permission from the author or the publisher.

Under no circumstances will any blame or legal responsibility be held against the publisher, or author, for any damages, reparation, or monetary loss due to the information contained within this book. Either directly or indirectly.

Legal Notice:

This book is copyright protected. This book is only for personal use. You cannot amend, distribute, sell, use, quote or paraphrase any part, or the content within this book, without the consent of the author or publisher.

Disclaimer Notice:

Please note the information contained within this document is for educational and entertainment purposes only. All effort has been executed to present accurate, up to date, and reliable, complete information. No warranties of any kind are declared or implied. Readers acknowledge that the author is not engaging in the rendering of legal, financial, medical or professional advice. The content within this book has been derived from various sources. Please consult a licensed professional before attempting any techniques outlined in this book.

By reading this document, the reader agrees that under no circumstances is the author responsible for any losses, direct or indirect, which are incurred as a result of the use of the information contained within this document, including, but not limited to, — errors, omissions, or inaccuracies.

TABLE OF CONTENTS

CHAPTER 1: INTRODUCTION

We would like to personally thank you for taking the time to purchase our book, The Christmas Jokes for Kids Book. We've spent countless hours putting together only the best silly, goofy and funny holiday jokes for you, the kids and the family to enjoy at any Christmas party! You can expect to find 250+ high quality hand picked holiday jokes.

CHAPTER 2: WHY JOKES?

This ultimate assortment of jokes for kids, family and friends will not only make you laugh but do so in a fun and interactive way. Jokes have been around since the dawn of time and have many other benefits such as:

-Confidence Boosting: *With so many kids and people in general struggling with self-confidence in our day and age, listening and interacting with these jokes in a safe environment with family and friends gives them the opportunity to comfortably say answers and repeat hilarious jokes, giving them the ability to not be afraid to express themselves.*

-Relieve Stress: *Jokes help in relieving your anger, depression, tension and stress and make you feel light and irritation free. It also improves the mood by reducing anxiety and fear. Laughter increases heart* *rate and blood pressure, both of which cools down your stress response.*

*-**Improved Bonding:** The Christmas Jokes for Kids Book is one of the best ways for friends and family to spend time with each other and build positive, healthy relationships through laughter and participation when listening to the jokes and trying to answer the questioning ones.*

*-**Personal Health:** Jokes make us laugh and impacts the body in a very positive way. When you start to laugh, it not only lightens your body but also induces many physical changes in it as well. Not only that, but funny jokes boost up the human immune system by increasing infection fighting antibodies.*

*-**Reduce Boredom:** Having an audiobook such as The Christmas Jokes for Kids Book gives you the ability to have fun and entertainment on demand. Since we provide it in audiobook form, it gives you the opportunity to utilize it in any situation!*

-Develop Humor: *Jokes sharpen your sensibilities and tune our capabilities. It improves your personality by bringing out your lighter side. Humor also allows people to express their feelings without any hesitation.*

Now, that's enough talking. Are you ready to get started with *The Christmas Jokes for Kids Book.*

Awesome! Let's Begin.

CHAPTER 3: JOKES

1. What do Santa's elves learn in school?

Answer: The Elf-abet!

2.   What does Santa like to do in the garden?

Answer: Hoe! Hoe! Hoe!

3.   What breakfast cereal does Frosty the Snowman eat?

Answer: Frosted Snowflakes!

4.   What type of cars do elves drive?

Answer: Toy-otas!

5.   Why did the Christmas tree go to the barber?

Answer: It needed a trim!

6.   What kind of motorcycle does Mrs. Claus ride?

Answer: A Holly Davidson!

7.   What do you call a bankrupt Santa?

Answer: Saint Nickel-less

8.   What do cats and dogs call Santa Clause?

Answer: Santa Paws!

9.   What do you get when you cross a Christmas tree with an apple?

Answer: A pine-apple!

10.   What do you get from a cow at the North Pole?

Answer: Ice Cream!

11.   Why do mummys like the holidays?

Answer: Because of all of the wrapping!

12.   Why don't aliens celebrate Christmas?

Answer: Becuase they don't want to give away their presence!

13.   Why does everybody like Frosty the Snowman?

Answer: Because he is so cool!

14.   Where are most of Santa's elves from?
Answer: Mini-sota!

15.   Where does the snowman hide his money?

Answer: In the snow bank of course!

16.   How did the ornament get addicted to Christma

Answer: He was hooked on the tree his whole life!

17.   Why is the Grinch so good at baseball?

Answer: He hits a lot of gnome runs!

18.   Why did Frosty ask for a divorce?

Answer: His wife was a total flake!

19.   Why does Scrooge love reindeer so much?

Answer: Because every single buck is deer to him!

20.   How much did Santa pay for his sleigh?

Answer: Nothing! Because it was on the house!

21.   What nationality is Santa Claus?

Answer: North Polish!

22.   What do you call a blind reindeer?

Answer: I have no eye-deer!

23.   What do you call an obnoxious reindeer?

Answer: Rude-olph!

24.   What's every elf's favorite type of music?

Answer: Wrap!

25.   What's the absolute best Christmas present?

Answer: A broken drum! You can't beat it…

26.   What do reindeers say before they tell you a joke?

Answer: "Are you sure you're ready? This is gunna sleigh you!"

27.   What did Adam say to his wife on Christmas?

Answer: It's finally Christmase, Eve!

28.   What's the difference between the Christmas alphabet and the ordinary alphabet?

Answer: The Christmas alphabet has no-el!!

29.   How do you know when Santa's around?

Answer: You can always sense his presents

30.   What do you call an elf that can sing and dance?

Answer: Elfis!

31.   What's every parent's favorite Christmas Carol?

Answer: Silent night!

32.   What does Santa suffer from if he gets stuck in a chimney?

Answer: Claus-trophobia!

33.   Who delivers presents to baby sharks at Christmas?

Answer: Santa Jaws!

34.   What happened to the man who stole an Advent Calendar?

Answer: He got 25 days

35.   Why couldn't the skeleton go to the Christmas party?

Answer: He had no-body to go with!

36.   What do they sing at a snowman's birthday party?

Answer: Freeze a jolly good fellow!

37.   Why was the turkey in the band?

Answer: Because he was the only one with drumsticks!

38.   What do snowmen wear on their heads?

Answer: Ice caps!

39.   What did the stamp say to the Christmas card?

Answer: "Stick with me and we will go places!"

40.   Why is Santa never sick?

Answer: Because he values his elf-care so much!

41.   How did Scrooge win the football game?

Answer: the ghost of Christmas Passed!

42.   What does Miley Cyrus have at Christmas?

Answer: Twerky!

43.   Why did Santa's helper see the doctor?

Answer: Because he had low elf-esteem!

44.   How do snowmen get around?

Answer: They ride an icicle!

45.   What's green, covered in tinsel and goes ribbet ribbet?

Answer: A mistle toad!

46.   What do reindeer hang on their Christmas trees?

Answer: Horn-aments!

47.   What happened to the turkey at Christmas?

Answer: It gets gobbled!

48.   What do you call a cat on the beach on Christmas Day?

Answer: Sandy-claws!!

49.   Why is Santa so good at karate?

Answer: Because he has a black belt!

50.   Where does mistletoe go to get famous?

Answer: Holy-wood!

51.   How do sheep say Merry Christmas in Mexico?

Answer: "Fleece Navidad!"

52.   Why did the turkey cross the road?

Answer: Because it was the chickens day off!

53.   What's Santa's favorite candy?

Answer: Jolly ranchers!

54.   What do you call a snowman that can drive?

Answer: A snow-mobile!

55.   What do you call a frog hanging from the ceiling?

Answer: A mistle-toad!

56.   What is Santa's favourite place to deliver presents?

Answer: Idaho-ho-ho!

57.   How does Darth Vader enjoy his Christmas Turkey?

Answer: on the dark side!

58.   Who's Rudolph's favourite pop star?

Answer: Beyon-sleigh!

59.   What do monkeys sing at Christmas?

Answer: Jungle Bells!

60.   Who is a Christmas tree's favorite singer?

Answer: Spruce Springsteen!

61.   How do you lift a frozen car?

Answer: With a jackfrost!

62.   What would you call an elf who just has won the lottery?

Answer: Very welfy!

63.   What do you call cutting down a Christmas tree?

Answer: Christmas chopping!

64.   Where do Santa and his reindeer go to get hot chocolate while flying in the sky?

Answer: Star-buck!

65.   What athlete is warmest in winter?

Answer: A long jumper!

66.   Why are Christmas trees so bad at sewing?

Answer: Because they always drop their needles!

67.   Why are Santa's deers always wet?

Answer: Because they're reindeers!

68.   What's a dinosaur's least favourite reindeer?

Answer: Comet!

69.   What do you call an elf who sings?

Answer: A wrapper

70.   Who does Santa call when his sleigh breaks down?

Answer: The Abominable Towman!

71.   Where do Santa's workers go when they are in need of counselling?

Answer: An elf-help group!

72.   What did Frosty's girlfriend give him when she was mad at him?

Answer: The cold shoulder!

73.   Who brings presents to all the good little crabs and lobsters at the beach?

Answer: Sandy Claws!

74.   What says 'oh oh oh'?

Answer: Santa walking backwards!

75.   Who is Santa's favourite singer?

Answer: Elfis Presely!

76.   What did Santa say to the smoker?

Answer: "Please don't smoke! It is bad for my personal elf!"

77.   Why did the Rudolph cross the road?

Answer: Because he was tied to the chicken!

78.   What carol is heard in the desert?

Answer: O Camel ye Faithful!

79.   What are the best Christmas sweaters made from?

Answer: Fleece Navidad!

80.   What do you get if you eat Christmas decorations?

Answer: You get Tinsilitus!

81.   How many elves does it take to change a light bulb?

Answer: 10! One to do the job and another 9 to stand on each others shoulders!

82.   What does Santa say to the toys on Christmas Eve?

Answer: "Okay everyone, sack time!"

83.   What does the gingerbread man put on his bed?

Answer: Cookie sheets!

84.   How does a snowman lose weight?

Answer: He waits for the weather to get warmers

85.   Why does Santa work at the North Pole?

Answer: Because the penguins kicked him out of the south pole!

86.   What do you call a reindeer who wears earmuffs?

Answer: Anything you want! They can't hear you!

87.   What do you get when you cross a snowman with a vampire?

Answer: Frostbite!

88.   Why did the Christmas tree go to the barber?

Answer: It needed to be trimmed!

89.   What do road crews use at the North Pole?

Answer: Snow cones!

90.   If an athlete gets athlete's foot, what does an astronaut get?

Answer: Missle Toe!

91.   Who delivers Christmas presents to elephants?

Answer: Elephanta claus!

92.   What do you call Santa if he goes down a lit chimney?

Answer: Crisp Cringle!

93.   How many presents can Santa fit in an empty sack?

Answer: Only one - after 1, it's not empty anymore!

94.   Why is it always cold at Christmas?

Answer: Because it is in Decembrrrrr

95.   When does Christmas come before Thanksgiving?

Answer: In the dictionary!

96.   How do elves get to the top floor of Santa's workshop?

Answer: They use the elfevator!

97.   How did Santa describe the elf who refuses to take a bath?

Answer: He's elfully smelly!

98.   What do sheep say to each other at Christmas?

Answer: Merry Christmas to Ewe!

99.   What happened to the thief who stole a Christmas calendar?

Answer: He got 12 months!

100.   What color Christmas candle burns longer, a red candle or a green candle?

Answer: Neither! A candle always burns shorter!

101.   What was the elf allergic to?

Answer: Sh-ELF-ish

102.   Who delivers Christmas gifts to Luke Skywalker?

Answer: Star Clause

103.   Who hides in the bakery during Christmas?

Answer: A mince spy!

104.   What goes ho-ho whoosh, ho-ho whoosh?

Answer: Santa caught in a revolving door!

105.   What did the lion at the beach have in common with Christmas?

Answer: Sandy claws!

106.   What do zombies put on their Christmas turkey?

Answer: Grave-y

107.   Who delivers Christmas presents to dogs?

Answer: Santa Paws!

108.   What do you call Santa Claus when he doesn't move?

Answer: Santa Pause!

109.   What type of potato chip is Santa's favorite?

Answer: Crisp Pringles!

110.   What falls at the North Pole but never gets hurt?

Answer: Snow!

111.   What do you get when you cross Santa Claus with a detective?

Answer: Santa Clues!

112.   Why couldn't the butterfly go to the Christmas party?

Answer: It was a moth ball!

113.   What is Santa's favorite Olympic event?

Answer: The North Pole-Vault

114.   What is green, white, and red all over?

Answer: A sunburnt elf!

115.   Why do reindeer tell such good stories?

Answer: Because they have all of the tails!

116.   How do you make a slow reindeer fast?

Answer: You don't feed it!

117.   Whats the best thing to put into a Christmas pie?

Answer: Your teeth!

118.   Why is Santa so jolly?

Answer: Because he knows where all of the toys are!

119.   What did the cow say on Christmas morning?

Answer: Moooooooey Christmas!

120.   What never eats at Christmas dinner?

Answer: The turkey because it's sutffed!

121.   What did the bald man say when he got a comb for Christmas?

Answer: Thank you! I will never part with it.

122.   When should you feed reindeer milk to a baby?

Answer: When it's a baby reindeer!

123.   If a reindeer lost his tail, where would it go for a new one?

Answer: A re-TAIL shop!

124.   What do you call it when Cris Kringle claps his hands?

Answer: Santapplause!

125.   What song did the guests sing at the Eskimo's Christmas party?

Answer: Freeze a jolly good fellow!

126.   What's black, white and red all over?

Answer: Santa Clause after he comes down the chimney!

127.   What did Mrs. Claus say to Santa Claus when she looked up in the sky?

Answer: "It looks like it might rein, deer!"

128.   What kinds of bug hates Christmas?

Answer: A humbug!

129.   What did the reindeer say to the elf?

Answer: Nothing, silly! Reindeer can't talk!

130.   What comes at the end of Christmas Day?

Answer: A 'Y'!

131.   What did the mouse give the other mouse for Christmas?

Answer: a christ-mouse card!

132.   What did the Christmas tree say to the ornament?

Answer: "Are you tired of hanging around here yet?"

133.   What do you have in December that you don't have in any other month?

Answer: The letter 'D'!

134.   What is Count Dracula's Christmas story?

Answer: a fright before Christmas!

135. When does a reindeer have a trunk?

Answer: When they go on vacation!

136. Why was Santa angry at Christmas?

Answer: Because of the Grinch who stole Christmas!

137. Why does Santa have elves in his workshop?

Answer: Because the Seven Dwarfs were all booked up!

138. What does Frosty the Snowman hang on his Christmas tree?

Answer: Icicles!

139. Why did Santa cross the road?

Answer: To deliver presents!

140.   What's invisible and smells like milk and cookies?

Answer: Santa burps!

141.   Why did Santa put a clock in his sleigh?

Answer: Because he wanted to see time fly!

142.   What's a big as Santa but weighs nothing?

Answer: Santa's Shadow!

143.   Why does Santa use reindeer to pull his sleigh?

Answer: Because horses can't fly!

144.   Who's black and white and says "HO, HO, HO?"

Answer: A penguin dressed up as Santa Clause!

145.   What's the best thing to give your parents for the holidays?

Answer: A list of everything you want!

146.   What's a good holiday tip?

Answer: Don't catch snow flakes with your tongue until all of the birds have flown south for the winter!

147.   What do you call a snowman in the summer?

Answer: A puddle!

148.   What do you call an old snowman?

Answer: Water!

149.   Why did Frosty have a carrot in his nose?

Answer: Because he forgot where the refrigerator was!

150.   What did Frosty call his cow?

Answer: An Eski-moo!

151.   What did the snowman order at McDonalds ?

Answer: Icebergers with chilly sauce!

152.   What does Frosty's wife put on her face at night?

Answer: Cold Cream!

153.   What does a Snowman take when he gets sick?

Answer: A chill pill!

154.   Two snowmen were standing in a field, and one said to the other, "Can you smell carrot?"

Answer: "No, but I can taste coal!"

155.   What do Snowmen call their kids?

Answer: Chill-dren!

156.   Where do elves go to dance?

Answer: Snow-balls!

157.   Why did the snowman send his father to Siberia?

Answer: Because he wanted a frozen pop!

158.   What two letters of the alphabet do reindeer prefer?

Answer: I, C

159.   Mom, Can I have a dog for Christmas?

Answer: "No! You can have a turkey like everyone else!"

160.   What's red, white and blue at Christmas time?

Answer: A sad candy cane!

161.   What is the best kind of key to get at Christmas?

Answer: A turkey!

162.   What do you call an elf who steals gift wrap from the rich and gives it to the poor?

Answer: Ribbon Hood!

163.   What do you call a snowman with a six pack?

Answer: An Ab-dominal Snowman!

164.   What's St. Nicholas's favorite measurement in the metric system?

Answer: A santa-meter!

165.   How do Christmas angels greet each other?

Answer: "Halo!"

166.   What's red and white and falls down chimneys?

Answer: Santa klutz!

167.   What did the peanut butter say to the strawberry on Christmas?

Answer: "Tis the season to be jelly!"

168.   What's Jack Frost's favorite part of the school day?

Answer: Snow and tell!

169.   Why do Dasher and Dancer love coffee?

Answer: Because they are Santa's star bucks!

170.   Why did Scrooge keep a pet lamb?

Answer: Because it would say, "Baaahhh humbug!"

171.   Where do you find reindeer?

Answer: It depends on where you leave them!

172.   Why didn't Rudolph get a good report card?

Answer: Because he went down in history!

173.   Why did the couple get engaged on the 24th of December?

Answer: So they could have a married Christmas!

174.   Why are Christmas trees so fond of the past?

Answer: Because the present is beneath them!

175.   What do you call a kid who doesn't believe in Santa?

Answer: a rebel without a clause!

176.   How does Santa keep his bathroom tiles immaculate?

Answer: He uses comet!

177.   What do the elves say to Santa when he's taking attendance at elf school?

Answer: "Present!"

178.   Why is Christmas such a good time?

Answer: Because everyone gets santa-mental!

179.   Why did Santa bring 22 reindeer to Walmart?

Answer: Because what he wanted to buy cost around 20 bucks, but just in case it was more, he brought some extra doe.

180.   Why does Santa go down the chimney?

Answer: Because it soots him!

181.   Where does Santa stay when he's on vacation?

Answer: At a ho - ho - hotel!

182.   How does Santa sing the alphabet?

Answer: A B C D E F G... H I J K L M N Oh!, Oh!, Oh!, P Q R S T...

183.   What do you call people who are afraid of Santa Claus?

Answer: Clause-trophobic

184.   Why did Santa get a parking ticket last Christmas Eve?

Answer: He left his sleigh in a SNOW parking zone!

185.   Why did the elf go to bed in the fireplace?

Answer: Because he wanted to sleep like a log

186.   Why does everyone like Frosty the Snowman?

Answer: Because he is so cool!

187.   What did one snowman say to the other snowman?

Answer: Have an ice day!

188.   What does Santa eat for breakfast?

Answer: Ice Krispies!

189.   What do reindeer hang on their Christmas tree?

Answer: Horn-aments!

190.   What kind of Christmas songs do fish like?

Answer: Christmas corals!

191.   What did the cow get for Christmas?

Answer: A cow-culator!

192.   What do you get if you cross mistletoe and a duck?

Answer: A Christmas quacker!

193.   Why did Jimmy's grades drop after the holidays?

Answer: Because everything was marked down!

194.   Why didn't the wig get any presents on Christmas?

Answer: Because he was very knotty!

195.   What does Santa say in a race?

Answer: "Ready, set, HO!"

196.   What two countries should the chef use when he's making Christmas dinner?

Answer: Turkey and Greece!

197.   Who is Frosty's favorite aunt?

Answer: Aunt Arctica!

198.   Where did Santa Claus go for vacation?

Answer: Santa Cruz

199.   What is a reindeer's favorite instrument?

Answer: A horn!

200.   How do you scare a snowman?

Answer: A heat gun!

201.   What's red and white, red and white, red and white?

Answer: Santa rolling down a snow bank!

202.   What comes before Christmas Eve?

Answer: Christmas Adam!

203.   What's white and red and goes up and down and up and down?

Answer: Santa Clause in an elevator!

204.　What do snowmen do on Christmas?

Answer: Hangout with snow angels!

205.　Did you hear about the cracker's Christmas party?

Answer: It was a bang!

206.　What did the reindeer say when he saw an elf?

Answer: Nothing, reindeer can't talk silly!

207.　What flies when it's born, lies when it's alive, and runs when it's dead?

Answer: A snowflake!

208.　What's white and goes up?

Answer: A confused snowflake!

209.   How do fish celebrate Christmas?

Answer: they hang reefs on their doors!

210.   What do elves like to do at the weekend?

Answer: Chill out!

211.   What do elves do after school?

Answer: Their gnome work!

212.   What do you get if you cross a bell with a skunk?

Answer: Jingle Smells!

213.   Why is it getting harder to buy Advent calendars?

Answer: Because their days are numbered!

214.   What's the most popular Christmas wine?

Answer: "I don't like brussel sprouts!"

215.   What did the snowman say to the aggressive carrot?

Answer: "Get out of my face!"

216.   What do you call a snowman on rollerblades?

Answer: A snowmobile!

217.   What did the beaver say to the Christmas tree?

Answer: "It's been nice gnawing you!"

218.   What's a mathematician's favorite Christmas snack?

Answer: Mince pi!

219.   Did Rudolph the red nosed reindeer go to school?

Answer: Nope! He was elf-taught!

220.   What did the snowflake say to the fallen leaf?

Answer: "You're so last season!"

221.   Why is a foot a good Christmas present?

Answer: Because it makes for a good stocking filler!

222.   What's the Abominable Snowman's favorite lunch?

Answer: An ice-burger!

223.   Where do they make movies about Christmas trees?

Answer: In Tinsel Town!

224.   How do you decorate a canoe for Christmas?

Answer: With oar-naments!

225.   What's Santa's tax status?

Answer: Elf-employed!

226.   Why does Santa owe everything to the elves?

Answer: Because he is an elf-made man!

227.   What's a female elf called?

Answer: A shelf!

228.   What's an elf's favorite type of cookie?

Answer: A short-bread cookie!

229.   Why do elves make good listeners?

Answer: Because they are all ears!

230.   Why do none of the elves names begin with 'S'?

Answer: Because that would be s-elfish!

231.   How do Santa's elves greet each other?

Answer: "Small world, isn't it?"

232.   What kind of money is used by Santa?

Answer: Jingle bills!

233.   What do you call an elf walking backwards?

Answer: A Fle!

234.   What do you call Santa's helpers?

Answer: Subordinate clauses!

235.   Knock, knock!
Who's there?
Noah.
Noah who?
Noah good Christmas joke?

236.   Knock, knock!
Who's there?
Chris.
Chris who?

Christmas is here!

237.   Knock, knock!
Who's there?
Coal.
Coal who?
Coal me when Santa's on his way.

238.   Knock, knock!
Who's there?
Gladys.
Gladys who?
Gladys Christmas. Aren't you too?

239.   Knock, knock!
Who's there?
Yah.
Yah who?
Wow, you're really excited about Christmas!

240.   Knock, knock!
Who's there?
Santa.
Santa who?
Santa Christmas card to you. Did you get it?

241.   Knock, knock!
Who's there?
Interrupting Santa.
Inter–
Ho ho ho! Merry Christmas!

242.   Knock, knock!
Who's there?
Howard.
Howard who?
Howard you like to sing Christmas carols with me?

243.   Knock, knock!
Who's there?
Anna.
Anna who?
Anna partridge in a pear tree.

244.   Knock, knock
Who's there?
Gladis
Gladis who?
Gladis not me who got coal this Christmas!

245.   Knock, Knock
Who's there?
Yule
Yule who?
Yule have fun during the holidays!

246.   Knock, knock!
Who's there?
Ima.
Ima who?

Ima dreaming of a white Christmas...

247.   Knock, knock!
Who's there?
Oh, Chris.
Oh, Chris who?
Oh Christmas tree, Oh Christmas tree...

248.   Knock, knock!
Who's there?
Freeze.
Freeze who?
Freeze a jolly good fellow. Freeze a jolly good
fellow...

249.   Knock, knock!
Who's there?
Elf.
Elf who?
Elf me wrap this present!

250.   Knock, Knock
Who's there?
Orange
Orange who?
Orange you glad you were good all year?

251.   Knock, Knock
Who's there?

Irish
Irish who?
Irish you a Merry Christmas!

252.   Knock, Knock
Who's there?
Mary
Mary who?
Marry Christmas!

253.   Knock, Knock
Who's there?
Donut
Donut who?
Donut open your presents until Christmas!

254.   Knock, knock
Who's there?
Snow
Snow who?
Snow use, I've forgotten my name!

CHAPTER 4: CONCLUSION

Wow! You made it through all 300 of the hilarious Christmas themed jokes this book.... How did they go? Did you have fun? These jokes have all been hand picked in order to make you laugh like there's no tomorrow! We hope you enjoyed going through them and they created some great memories between you, your friends and your family.

Once again, we would like to thank you for reading our book *The Christmas Jokes for Kids Book* and we can't wait to hear what you thought about it. If you enjoyed listening to this book, please don't forget to leave a review and let us know exactly how much you loved it. Reviews mean the world to us and help us continue to create books just like this one for years to come.

Happy holidays and Merry Christmas to you!

DL Digital Entertainment

Made in the USA
Monee, IL
16 December 2019

18785010R00037